CONTENTS

WHAT A LOAD OF RUBBISH

Every year, we throw away more rubbish than ever before. The type of rubbish has also changed. Fifty years ago there was far more dust and cinders, and no plastic at all. Nowadays, the average family throws away 600 cans, 2 trees' worth of paper, 120 plastic bottles, and 2.4 kg of plastic wrapping, 449 glass bottles and jars and 24 kg of rags.

We don't need to throw away so much. By making a few changes in the way we live we can save money and energy, and help to protect our environment.

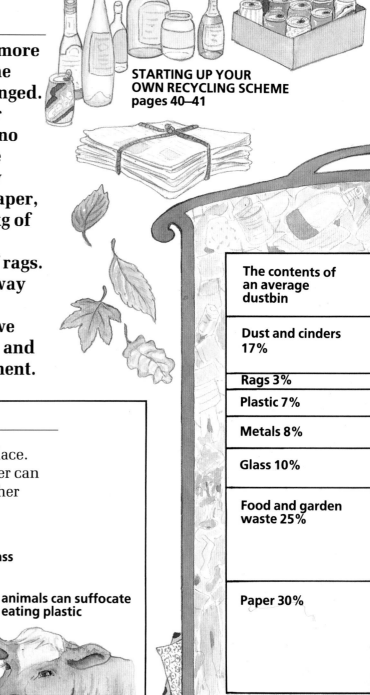

STARTING UP YOUR OWN RECYCLING SCHEME pages 40–41

The contents of an average dustbin

Dust and cinders 17%

Rags 3%

Plastic 7%

Metals 8%

Glass 10%

Food and garden waste 25%

Paper 30%

LITTER

Litter is rubbish in the wrong place. Apart from being unsightly, litter can be dangerous to humans and other animals.

cuts from broken glass

animals can suffocate eating plastic

trapped birds cannot fly or feed

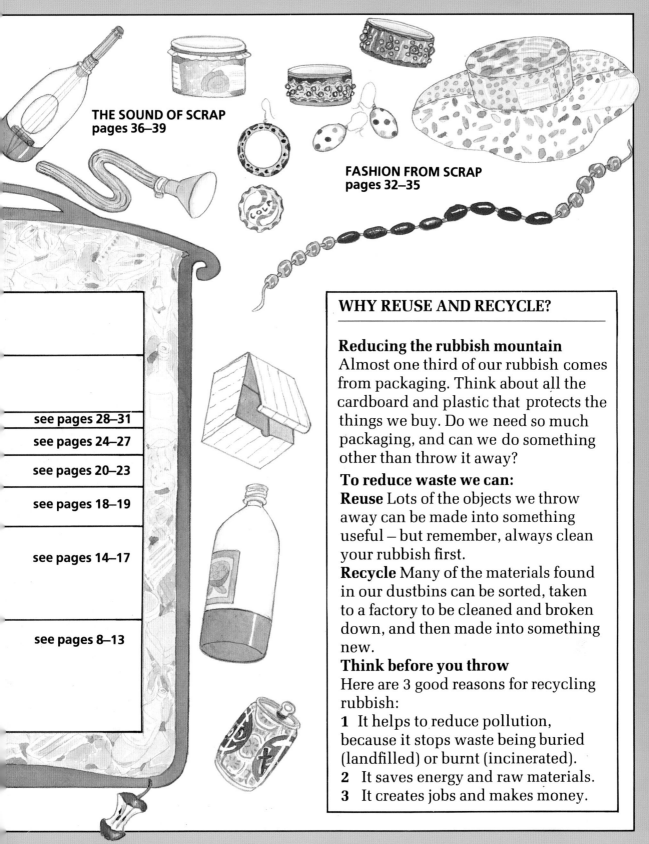

THE SOUND OF SCRAP
pages 36–39

FASHION FROM SCRAP
pages 32–35

WHY REUSE AND RECYCLE?

Reducing the rubbish mountain
Almost one third of our rubbish comes from packaging. Think about all the cardboard and plastic that protects the things we buy. Do we need so much packaging, and can we do something other than throw it away?

To reduce waste we can:
Reuse Lots of the objects we throw away can be made into something useful – but remember, always clean your rubbish first.
Recycle Many of the materials found in our dustbins can be sorted, taken to a factory to be cleaned and broken down, and then made into something new.

Think before you throw
Here are 3 good reasons for recycling rubbish:
1 It helps to reduce pollution, because it stops waste being buried (landfilled) or burnt (incinerated).
2 It saves energy and raw materials.
3 It creates jobs and makes money.

PAPER

About 30% of our rubbish is paper or cardboard. We use much more today than we used to, and some countries use far more paper than others. The paper we use comes from waste paper that has been recycled, and from forests in Europe, particularly Scandinavia. Sometimes when trees are cut down to make paper, the forests are replanted with different trees that do not attract the same variety of wildlife as before.

SAVING ENERGY AND TREES

To make new, or "virgin" paper, trees are cut down, and their branches and bark are removed. About 2 tonnes of wood and 200,000 litres of water are used to make 1 tonne of paper – that's about 10–17 trees (enough for 7,000 copies of a national newspaper). It takes more energy to produce virgin paper than recycled paper. If we recycle our paper, we are reducing waste, saving forests and the habitats of wildlife in the forests.

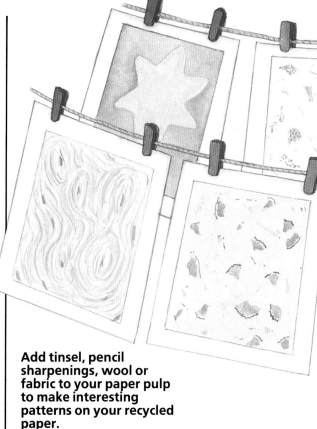

Add tinsel, pencil sharpenings, wool or fabric to your paper pulp to make interesting patterns on your recycled paper.

Reductions (%) made when recycling paper instead of producing virgin paper

35% water pollution

48% energy

58% water use

74% air pollution

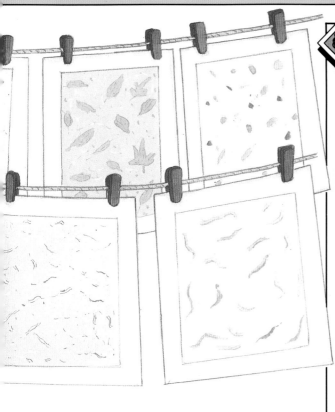

By keeping your own record of paper collection you can see how much money you are saving. Your notebook can be used for your other recycled items too.

MAKE A MASK

WHAT YOU NEED

25cm

25cm

piece of card

scissors

old newspapers and colour magazines

bucket of wallpaper paste

How to make it

1 Draw a sketch of your mask on the card. Tear the newspaper into strips and roll them in the paste.

2 Make each one into a sausage shape and lay them on the card. You can mould the face like clay. Wash your hands – they'll get very wet and sticky!

3 Use magazines to find coloured paper for your mask – a tiger will need lots of yellow, orange and black. Stick the coloured squares onto your mask, filling in the whole face – it's like making up a jigsaw puzzle.

4 Leave the mask until it is dry. You can then cut out your mask.

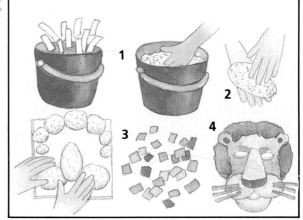

9

A CLOSER LOOK

There are 11 grades of waste paper used for recycling. High-grade papers include computer paper and stationery. High-grade paper is more valuable and easier to recycle than low-grade paper. This is because it has longer fibres that mesh together more easily. It also has less impurities, such as ink, glue and wax which need to be removed. This is why glossy magazines and telephone directories are difficult to recycle.

Low-grade papers are reused where colour and quality are not so important. They include newspaper and packaging materials such as cardboard boxes and cereal boxes.

You can examine examples of low-grade and high-grade papers with a magnifying glass. Lay some sticky tape on some newspaper and then pull it off so that strands or fibres of paper are left on it. If too much paper comes off, try again. Study the strands. Try this again with computer paper. Do these fibres look different?

MAKE YOUR OWN PAPER

WHAT YOU NEED

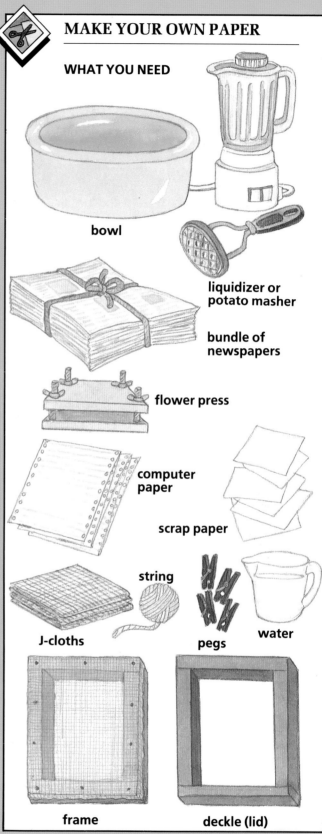

bowl

liquidizer or potato masher

bundle of newspapers

flower press

computer paper

scrap paper

string

J-cloths

pegs

water

frame

deckle (lid)

10

1 Tear up the computer paper and leave it to soak in water overnight.

2 Mash or liquidize (with an adult) the paper until it turns into pulp and looks like porridge.

3 Add more water and stir. Put the deckle on top of the frame and scoop some pulp into it. Lift out, draining the water from the frame.

4 Remove the deckle and put the frame, pulp side down, onto the J-cloth (like shutting a book). Wipe up any excess water and lift the frame off the paper pulp, leaving it on the J-cloth. Now place a piece of scrap paper on top.

5 If you are making more than one piece of paper, you can build up a "sandwich" of J-cloth, recycled paper and scrap paper. To squeeze out the last drops of water from the recycled paper, use the flower press, or put newspaper on top of your pile, take it outside and stand on it.

Hang the paper up to dry overnight (see pages 8/9) – you can then easily peel it off the scrap paper.

After lifting off your frame place a piece of scrap paper on top of the pulp.

pulp

HOW STRONG IS CARDBOARD?

We use cardboard for many kinds of packaging. But how strong is it? In the past furniture and houses have been made from papier mâché and cardboard. Do you think you could sit on a stool made from cardboard? Why not make one and see?

WHAT YOU NEED

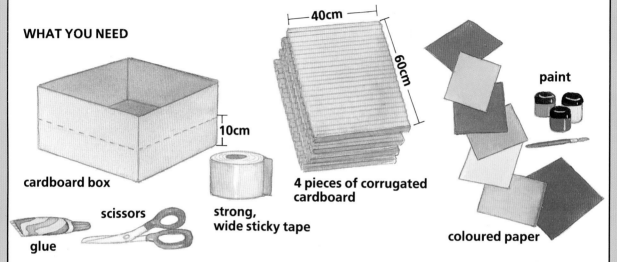

cardboard box

10cm

4 pieces of corrugated cardboard

40cm

60cm

paint

coloured paper

glue

scissors

strong, wide sticky tape

What to do

1 Trim the cardboard box to a depth of 10cm. Use the spare cardboard to strengthen the bottom of the box.
2 Roll 1 piece of cardboard into a column and secure it with tape. Do this with the other 3 pieces of card. These columns will be the legs.
3 Use the sticky tape and glue to secure the cardboard legs to each corner of the stool.
4 Decorate your stool with paint or coloured paper. Leave to dry.

Will the stool hold your weight? It should do if all the legs are even and have been firmly fastened to the corners of the box. Do you think an adult could sit on your stool?

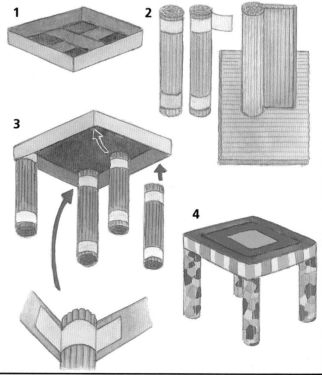

A PAPIER MÂCHÉ BOWL

WHAT YOU NEED:

wallpaper paste

small plastic bowl

coloured paper

varnish brush

Vaseline

1 Spread a thin layer of Vaseline on the outside of the plastic bowl to stop your papier mâché sticking once it has dried.

2 Decide on the design of your bowl. Tear the pieces of coloured paper to suit your design. Dip each piece into the paste and stick them on the outside of the bowl. The more layers you use, the tougher your new bowl will be.

3 Your bowl will need a few days to dry out, then ease it away from the plastic bowl.

4 Varnishing makes it tougher, but it still cannot be used as a cereal bowl. Why not?

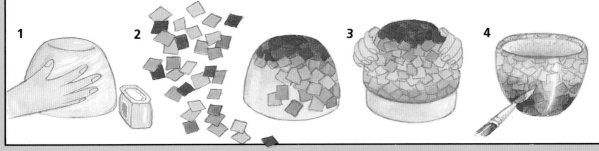

1   2   3   4

PAPER CHAINS

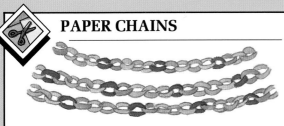

When we celebrate birthdays or Christmas, we can waste a lot of paper. We wrap our presents in paper and we also use it for our decorations and greeting cards. You can now buy cards and wrapping paper made from recycled paper. Also, by reusing old paper to make decorations we are cutting down on this waste. Why not make paper chains from old colour magazines or brightly coloured scrap paper?

DUSTBIN FACTS

A forest the size of Sweden has to be cut down every *year* to supply the world with the paper it uses. That's more than 3,000 trees a day!

In the USA, each person uses an average of 300 kg of paper every year. In Europe each person uses 200 kg, but in India the amount is only 6 kg.

In Japan, paper was being repulped and reused as early as the year 1035.

In 1897, a papermaker from Chicago introduced hard-wearing paper horseshoes.

FOOD AND GARDEN WASTE

Over 25% of the contents of an average dustbin is made up of food waste. Most kitchen and garden waste can be recycled into compost and used on flowerbeds or garden vegetable patches to improve the soil. It is best to vary what you put into your compost heap as this produces a good balanced source of food for your garden. Too much soft material, like grass cuttings, will end up mushy, and too much tough material, like prunings, will take a long time to rot.

DECOMPOSITION

Vegetable and animal waste is biodegradable. This means that it will rot in soil – it will be broken down into tiny pieces by bacteria.

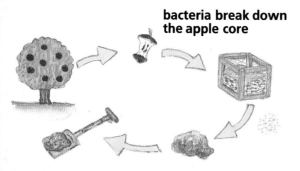

bacteria break down the apple core

compost will enrich the soil with nutrients and feed the apple tree

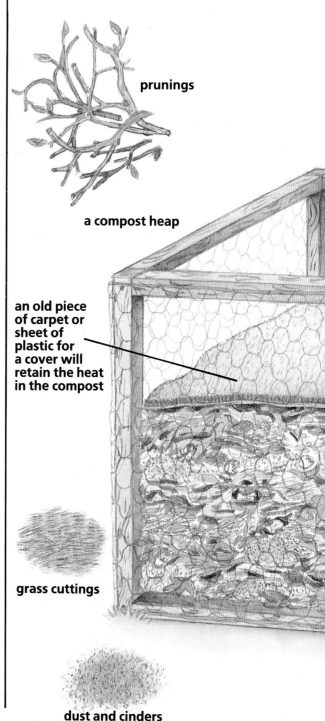

prunings

a compost heap

an old piece of carpet or sheet of plastic for a cover will retain the heat in the compost

grass cuttings

dust and cinders

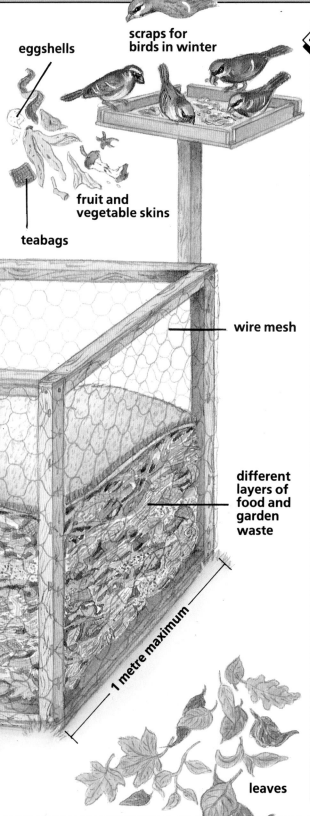

eggshells

scraps for birds in winter

fruit and vegetable skins

teabags

wire mesh

different layers of food and garden waste

1 metre maximum

leaves

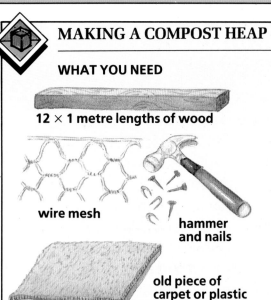

WHAT YOU NEED

12 × 1 metre lengths of wood

wire mesh

hammer and nails

old piece of carpet or plastic

1 Choose a corner in your garden – not too damp or sunny.
2 Ask an adult to nail the wood together to make the frame and then nail the wire mesh to the frame.
3 Add different layers, such as food and garden waste and dust and cinders, to your compost heap.
4 The organic waste will take about 6–9 months to rot down. The heap will decompose quickly, if it retains its heat, so add waste all at once, cover and leave.
5 Shovel the compost from the bottom of the heap.

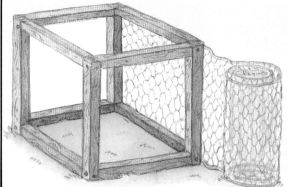

SPRING

Lots of seeds, pips and stones from food are thrown away after every meal. Collect some seeds, plant them in a small tub, water them, and see if they grow. An avocado or peach stone can be planted straight into the soil. Tomato and pepper seeds can be planted in seed trays 2 cm apart and later put into small pots or plastic cups.

SUMMER

WHAT YOU NEED

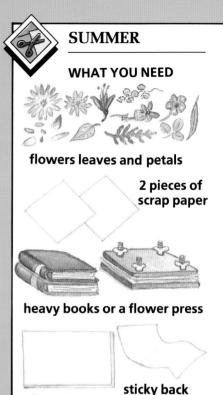

flowers leaves and petals

2 pieces of scrap paper

heavy books or a flower press

piece of card

sticky back plastic

AUTUMN

Deciduous trees lose all their leaves each Autumn. Some people think that fallen leaves on the ground are litter, but they provide the soil with nutrients. Go for a walk where there are lots of trees. Collect some of the fallen leaves, but **don't** pick any from the trees; this is illegal. Try to collect a wide range of colours. How many different shades can you find? Find a sheltered place to arrange your leaf rainbow, either indoors or outside. Are there any colours of the rainbow that you didn't find?

WINTER

Christmas decorations can be made from many types of materials including paper, plastic and metal. They can also be made from natural materials, like this pine cone wreath.

WHAT YOU NEED

fallen tree branches and twigs

string

red ribbon

cotton

white paint

found pine cones

Collect flowers, leaves and petals from the ground, or pick them from your own garden, and press them between two sheets of white paper for at least a week. You could make a picture, birthday card, badge, bookmark, or even use your flowers to decorate a papier mâché bowl, or your piece of recycled paper (see page 11). If you seal your leaves in sticky-back plastic, they will last for a long time.

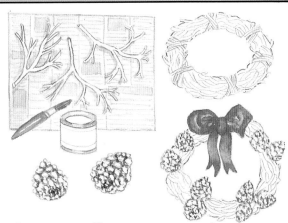

When you collect your natural materials, remember just take what you need and **only** take branches that are on the ground. Paint some twigs white. Entwine the twigs and branches into a circle, and secure with cotton. Then tie your pine cones around the wreath. Tie a red bow at the top of your decoration — you can use this to hang your wreath.

FOOD FROM SCRAPS

Scraps like fat, stale bread and apple cores can be a useful source of food for birds during winter. If you hang fat from a stick near rose bushes, this will attract blue tits, who will eat any wintering aphids and greenfly. Remember that you shouldn't feed birds during the spring time, because their young need food from their natural habitat.

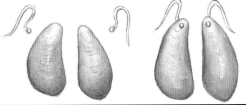

MUSSEL SHELL EARRINGS

Seafood shells can be thoroughly cleaned and used to make jewellery, eg. mussel shells can be made into earrings. Make a hole and attach some hoops that you can buy from a craft shop.

DUSTBIN FACTS

When organic waste rots, it produces a smelly gas called methane (CH_4). Methane is explosive and is also one of the gases responsible for global warming. Sometimes, when rubbish is buried in a landfill site, this gas can build up and cause explosions.

In the 1940s the city of St Petersburg was surrounded by its enemies, so the people were forced to make soup from leather shoes.

GLASS

About 10% of the contents of an average dustbin is glass. Thirty years ago, we used much more glass for packaging than we do today. Many of the bottles, jars and other containers bought at the shops were made of glass because there were no alternatives, like plastic. Think about all the glass bottles and jars you can collect and sort. Some can be recycled at the bottle bank, others can be rinsed and returned, and the rest could be reused.

RAW MATERIALS

Most of the raw materials used for making glass can be found in large quantities under the ground. However, if we reuse our glass, we're saving all the money and energy that we use to dig up sand and limestone. We are also generating less pollution. The raw materials for making glass are melted down in a furnace. Then, the bottles and jars are blown into shape. Less energy is required to melt down old broken glass, or cullet, than to melt down the raw materials for new glass.

sand (75%)

% needed for new glass

limestone (15%)

soda ash (10%)

Returnable bottles are made of thick glass and can be taken back to the shop where you bought them.

Recyclable bottles are called "one-trip containers" and can be taken to a bottle bank.

Jars can be reused for jam-making, or used to store dry foods, such as rice and pasta.

Glass is transparent so a jam jar can also be reused to make a lantern.

A GLASS LANTERN

WHAT YOU NEED

small candle

round glass jar

length of wire (70cm)

wallpaper paste

newspaper

paint

brush

How to make it

1 Wash the jar thoroughly. Taking care, make a handle with the wire, bending it around the lip of the jar, as shown.

2 Using the scrap sculpture method (see page 9), mould the paper and paste around the handle, and the bottom of the jar. Leave to dry for two days.

3 Decorate with paint. Put the candle at the bottom of the jar. Ask an adult for help if you want to light your candle.

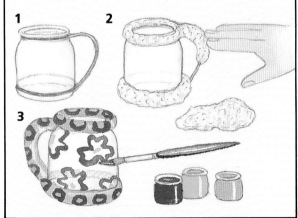

METALS

About 8% of our household rubbish is made up of metal cans. Cans have been used as food containers for over 150 years. The first cans were very thick and quite heavy. Today, they are much thinner and lighter because of improvements in technology. We can now make 7000 more cans from one tonne of metal than we could ten years ago.

MAKING NEW METAL

All metals have to be mined from under the ground. This is an expensive and dirty process. A great deal of energy, in the form of heat, is needed to turn bauxite into aluminium and iron ore into steel. This causes pollution. If we recycle steel cans, we save 75% of the energy required to make steel from iron ore. When we recycle our aluminium cans, we save 95% of the energy required.

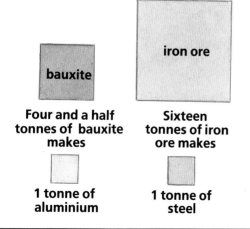

bauxite

iron ore

Four and a half tonnes of bauxite makes

Sixteen tonnes of iron ore makes

1 tonne of aluminium

1 tonne of steel

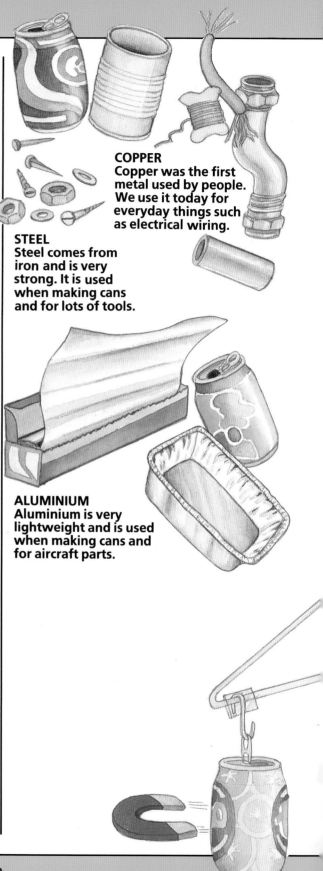

COPPER
Copper was the first metal used by people. We use it today for everyday things such as electrical wiring.

STEEL
Steel comes from iron and is very strong. It is used when making cans and for lots of tools.

ALUMINIUM
Aluminium is very lightweight and is used when making cans and for aircraft parts.

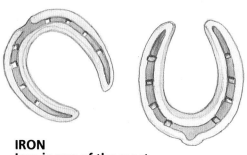

IRON
Iron is one of the most common metals. Iron ore makes up 5% of the Earth's outer shell.

WEIGHT BALANCE
If the cans balance, they are made of the same metal. If one can falls below the level of the other, it is heavier and therefore contains steel.

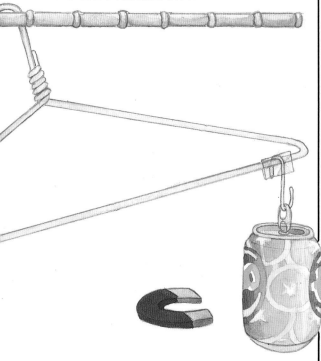

MAKE A WEIGHT BALANCE

WHAT YOU NEED

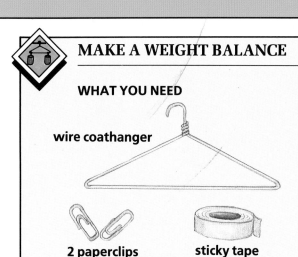

wire coathanger

2 paperclips   sticky tape

1 Pull the paperclips into an 'S' shape. Take care when you do this.
2 Hang the coathanger on the end of the cane. Can you balance it? Secure the paperclips on either side of the coathanger with the sticky tape, and check that it is still balanced. Each piece of tape will have to be the same size, and the clips should be secured the same distance from each end. Choose 2 cans which are the same size. Hang one on each paperclip. How can you identify the metal if the two cans balance? To find out more, see the next page.

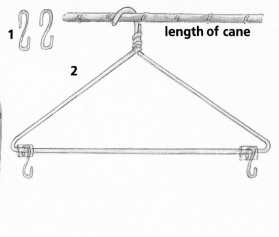

length of cane

IDENTIFYING METALS

Apart from testing cans for their weight, there are other ways of identifying what metals they are made of.

Is the can magnetic?
Steel cans are magnetic. Aluminium cans are not.

Does the can rust?
Steel cans rust in water. Aluminium cans do not. Inside the can is an anti- corrosive coating to stop it rusting. To test whether the can will rust, scrape it with a nail and leave in a bowl of salty water for approximately two days.

A JUMPING FROG

WHAT YOU NEED

piece of card

aluminium foil food tray

tape

scissors

paint or colouring pens

pencil

How to make it
1 Cut a long strip of foil from your food tray and wrap it around the pencil.
2 Pull the coil lengthways and roll it up again. This makes it springier.
3 Use the card and pens to design your frog and stick it on the top of the metal coil.
4 Push the coil down onto a table or hard surface and let go. The frog should leap into the air.

Why not ask your friends to make a jumping frog and hold a competition to see whose frog can jump the highest?

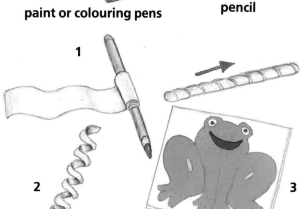

A LITTER BIN

Sculptors often use wire mesh as a frame onto which they add other materials. It is flexible, lightweight and easily moulded into any shape. Wire mesh is ideal as a frame for a litter bin.

WHAT YOU NEED

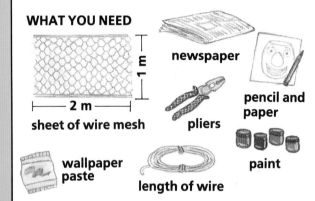

newspaper

1 m

2 m

sheet of wire mesh

pliers

pencil and paper

paint

wallpaper paste

length of wire

DUSTBIN FACTS

Seven million cans are thrown away in Britain every year — 4 and a half million of these are soft drinks cans. If these were laid end to end, they would stretch from one end of the country to the other.

In America 110 billion drinks cans are bought every year.

The world average recycling rate for aluminium cans is 50%; in Europe the figure is 20%.

Design a prototype of your bin first. This could be a small model of the finished design or a plan on paper. Think about where you are going to put your finished litter bin. An outdoor bin will need a lid, or need to be enclosed, to protect it from the wind and rain. Your bin could be used to collect cans, or other materials for recycling.

How to make it

1 Mould the wire mesh to the shape of the bin you would like. You may need an adult to help you at this stage. Fix the wire mesh skeleton together with small pieces of wire.
2 Using the scrap sculpture method (see page 9), cover the inside and the outside of the bin with pasted newspaper. It will take a few days to build up many layers, but this will make the bin strong.
3 Leave to dry for at least a week. If the weather is hot and sunny, your bin will take less time to dry.

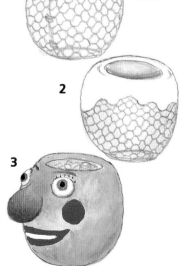

Now you can decorate the bin. Bright colours will make the bin stand out and so more people will use it. If the bin is going outside, you will need to varnish it to protect it in all weather conditions.

PLASTICS

Although plastics make up about 7% of our household waste by weight they take up 20% of the space in our dustbins. This is because they are so light. So if we measured the contents of our bins by volume, then plastics would make up one fifth of our household waste. The first man-made plastic was made by Leo Baekeland in 1908. Since then, many more plastics have been invented.

SORTING PLASTICS

Plastic is difficult to recycle, because there are so many different types. It is also expensive to sort and difficult to clean. But we can reuse plastics, and recycle where possible. This will reduce the oil and energy used to make plastic and that will help cut down on pollution.

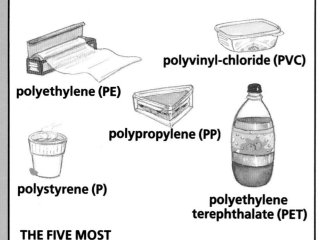

polyvinyl-chloride (PVC)

polyethylene (PE)

polypropylene (PP)

polystyrene (P)

polyethylene terephthalate (PET)

THE FIVE MOST COMMON TYPES OF PLASTIC

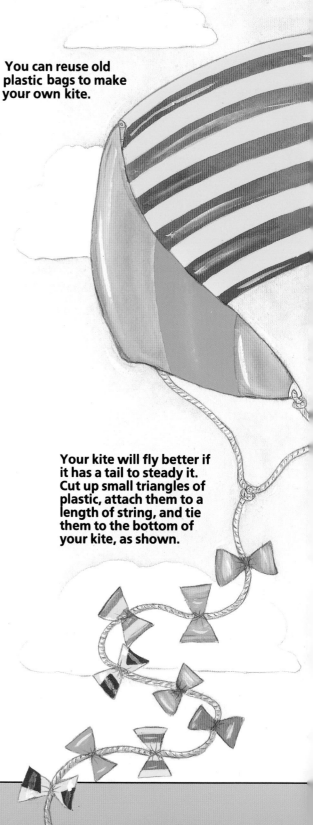

You can reuse old plastic bags to make your own kite.

Your kite will fly better if it has a tail to steady it. Cut up small triangles of plastic, attach them to a length of string, and tie them to the bottom of your kite, as shown.

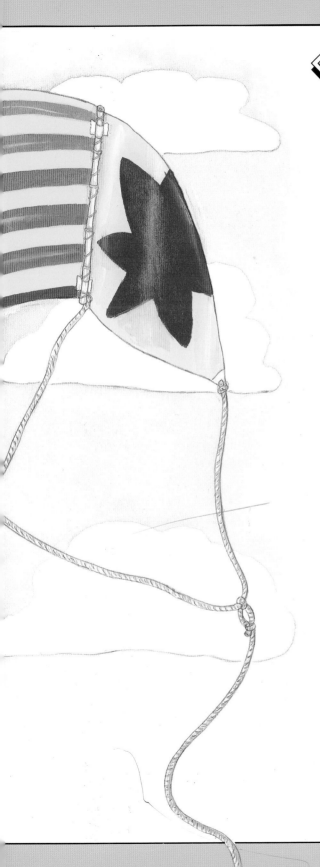

HOW TO MAKE A KITE

WHAT YOU NEED

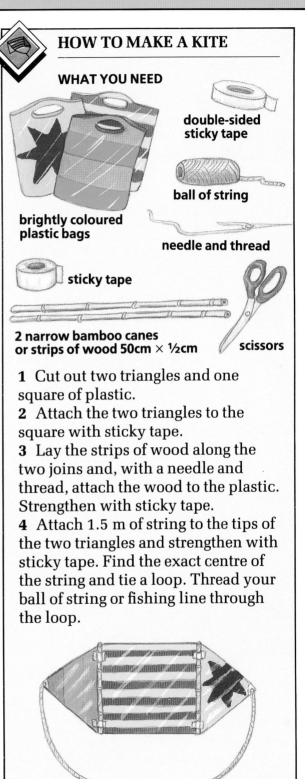

double-sided sticky tape

ball of string

brightly coloured plastic bags

needle and thread

sticky tape

2 narrow bamboo canes or strips of wood 50cm × ½cm

scissors

1 Cut out two triangles and one square of plastic.

2 Attach the two triangles to the square with sticky tape.

3 Lay the strips of wood along the two joins and, with a needle and thread, attach the wood to the plastic. Strengthen with sticky tape.

4 Attach 1.5 m of string to the tips of the two triangles and strengthen with sticky tape. Find the exact centre of the string and tie a loop. Thread your ball of string or fishing line through the loop.

REUSING A FIZZY DRINK BOTTLE

You can reuse a clear fizzy drink bottle in a number of ways.

A funnel or telephone

The top of the bottle can be used as a funnel. If you attach a piece of hose pipe or tubing to two funnels, you will have made a simple telephone.

A cloche

A cloche helps seedlings to grow by trapping sunlight. It can also protect young plants from being eaten by slugs or damaged by larger animals and humans who may tread or sit on them.

HMS RECYCLER

WHAT YOU NEED

3 elastic bands

margarine tub or plastic food tray

fizzy drink bottle

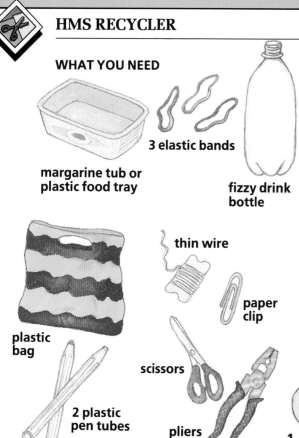

plastic bag

thin wire

paper clip

scissors

2 plastic pen tubes

pliers

1 To make the propeller, cut out the shape from your fizzy drink bottle. Make a hole in the centre of the plastic.
2 Attach one end of an elastic band to the piece of wire and attach a paperclip to the other end. Thread the wire through the pen tube, and then through the propeller. Bend the wire outwards so that it doesn't pull back through the pen.
3 Attach the propeller to the margarine tub with elastic bands. If you twist the propeller round and round, the elastic band will wind up. When you let go, it will spin around and power your boat.
4 Make a sail from an old plastic bag with a plastic pen tube for the mast.

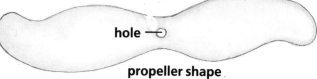

1

hole

propeller shape

A JELLY MOULD

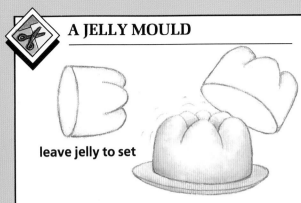

leave jelly to set

The bottom of a fizzy drink bottle makes an ideal jelly mould for one person. If you collect a few, you could have enough for a party! Before you turn out your jelly, dip your mould into hot water – this will make sure that the jelly comes out in one piece!

DUSTBIN FACTS

70% of the plastics found in Europe's dustbins come from packaging. A lot of oil and energy is used to make these containers – and they are only used once!

About 5 million plastic containers are thrown overboard from ships every day. Plastic debris can often be seen on the surface waters of the North Atlantic.

Sea turtles can starve to death by eating floating plastic, which they mistake for food. Their stomachs become filled with plastic and so there is no room for food.

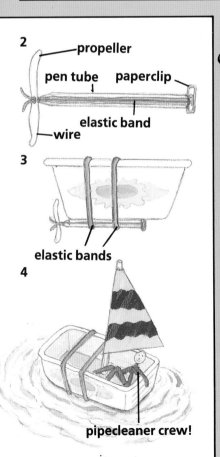

2
propeller
pen tube   paperclip
elastic band
wire

3
elastic bands

4
pipecleaner crew!

HOW LONG DOES PLASTIC LAST?

Plastics last and last. They don't even rot when they are buried in soil. This is because they are not biodegradable. See how indestructible plastic is by burying a small piece in a pot with an apple core. Compare what happens. You may have to wait a very long time to see a change in the piece of plastic.

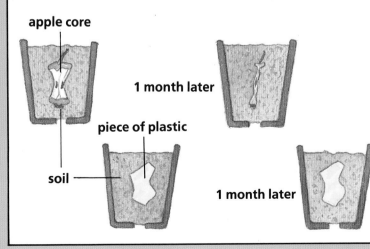

apple core

1 month later

piece of plastic

soil

1 month later

TEXTILES

Fabrics, or textiles, make up about 3% of our household waste. We can reuse old clothes by buying from and giving to charity shops and jumble sales. At home cotton clothes can be improved by printing or dyeing. Wool, which is particularly valuable, can be reused by unpicking old jumpers and knitting something new.

RAW MATERIALS

Textiles can be split into two groups: natural fibres which come from animals or plants such as wool and cotton, and synthetic or 'man-made' fibres such as nylon and polyester. Synthetic fibres should be recycled as this saves the oil that is used in making them.

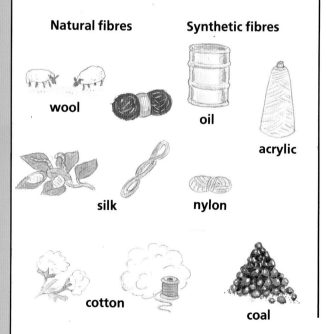

Natural fibres

wool

silk

cotton

Synthetic fibres

oil

acrylic

nylon

coal

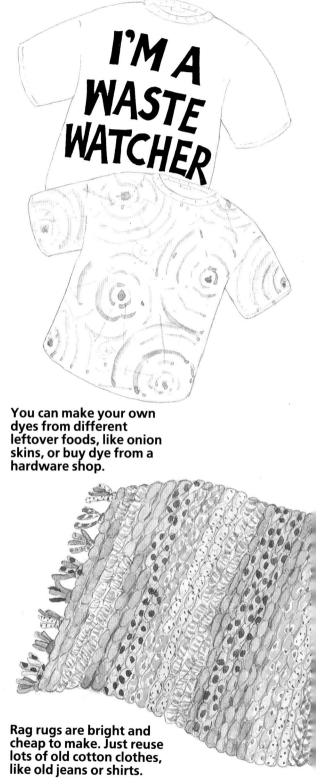

You can make your own dyes from different leftover foods, like onion skins, or buy dye from a hardware shop.

Rag rugs are bright and cheap to make. Just reuse lots of old cotton clothes, like old jeans or shirts.

You can buy a small loom from an art shop, but they are quite easy to make. You need a wooden frame with nails on either side.

MAKE A RAG RUG

WHAT YOU NEED

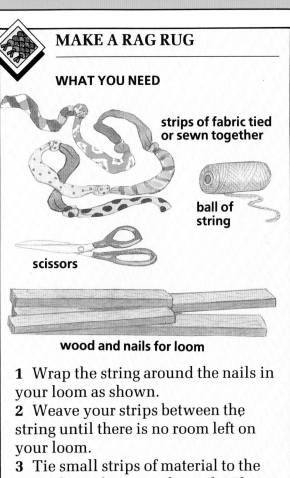

strips of fabric tied or sewn together

ball of string

scissors

wood and nails for loom

1 Wrap the string around the nails in your loom as shown.
2 Weave your strips between the string until there is no room left on your loom.
3 Tie small strips of material to the string loops between the nails. These form the fringe edges on your rug.
4 You can now carefully remove the finished rug from the loom.

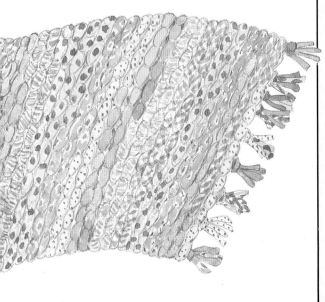

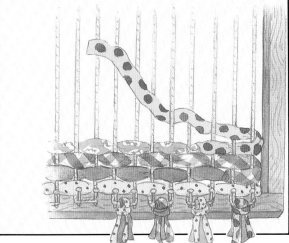

WEAVING CLOTH

Weaving is how cloth, or fabric, is made. If you look closely at a piece of cloth, you will see two sets of threads crossing each other. These are known as the weft and warp. The weft runs across and the warp runs down.

To create stripes in cloth, the colour of the weft is changed. You can use lots of different colours and materials for the weft – even strips of plastic bags!

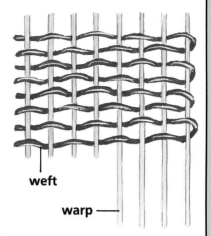

weft

warp

TRANSFORM A T-SHIRT

You can buy colour dyes from a department store or hardware shop. Remember to check with an adult before you start.

WHAT YOU NEED:

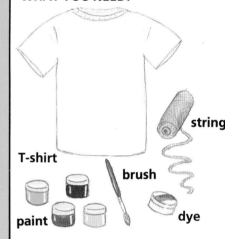

T-shirt

string

brush

paint

dye

REUSING RAGS

Patchwork quilts have been made for centuries as a way of reusing old material. Why not use this idea to make a rag bag? Cut scraps of fabric into squares. Sew the squares together to make two large squares of the same size. Sew these together and make a handle from other scraps.

Or why not use an old sock to make a hand puppet? Trim the top off your sock so that it fits over your hand and wrist. Put your hand in the sock to make the mouth.

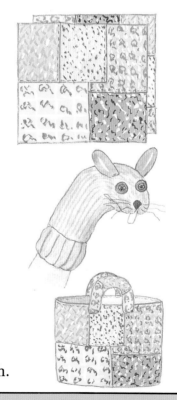

TRADE IN TEXTILES

Cotton is grown in hot countries like Africa, India and some parts of America. It is then sold to Europe as a cash crop.

Second-hand clothes can be of a high quality, so these are sorted and sold abroad. Cotton clothing is particularly useful for developing countries

and warmer clothes are sold to colder countries.

Blankets are made from old fabric and sent to countries hit by famine. They can be used as tents or clothing.

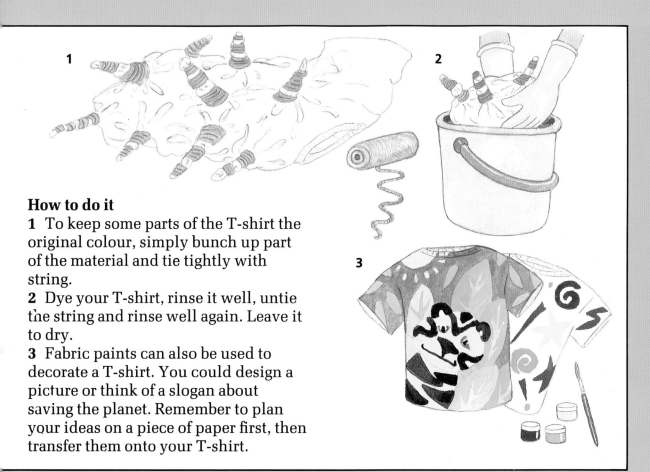

How to do it

1 To keep some parts of the T-shirt the original colour, simply bunch up part of the material and tie tightly with string.

2 Dye your T-shirt, rinse it well, untie the string and rinse well again. Leave it to dry.

3 Fabric paints can also be used to decorate a T-shirt. You could design a picture or think of a slogan about saving the planet. Remember to plan your ideas on a piece of paper first, then transfer them onto your T-shirt.

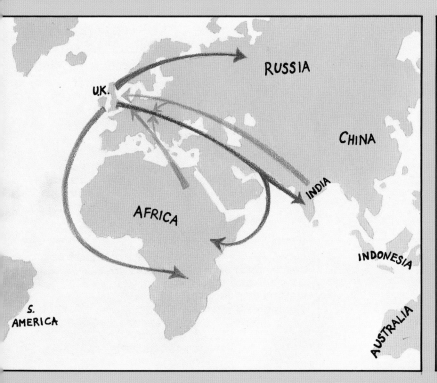

DUSTBIN FACTS

In Britain about 125,000 tonnes of rags are thrown away every year. That's like throwing £65 million straight into the dustbin.

Four thousand years ago the Ancient Egyptians used linen made from the flax plant to wrap dead bodies in.

FASHION FROM SCRAP

There are many ways to recycle and reuse materials such as plastic packaging, newspaper and wrappings to create colourful and unique accessories and clothing. Some famous fashion designers use scrap in their collections, and pop videos have included outfits made from rubbish.

If you use your imagination, you can make your own designs at little or no cost. Search out interesting pieces of rubbish. Sort your finds according to colour and texture, and see what uses their shapes suggest. A washing-up bottle may be used to make bangles and plastic bags can become hats!

FINDING IDEAS

Many artists working in this century have turned scrap materials into beautiful and interesting objects. Alexander Calder, for example, used scrap metal to make sculpture. Ask at the library for books about his and other artists' work.

Why not make a hat and "waste" coat to match?

Make a quick badge from a colourful metal bottle top by holding it against a T-shirt and pressing a button into the back through the material.

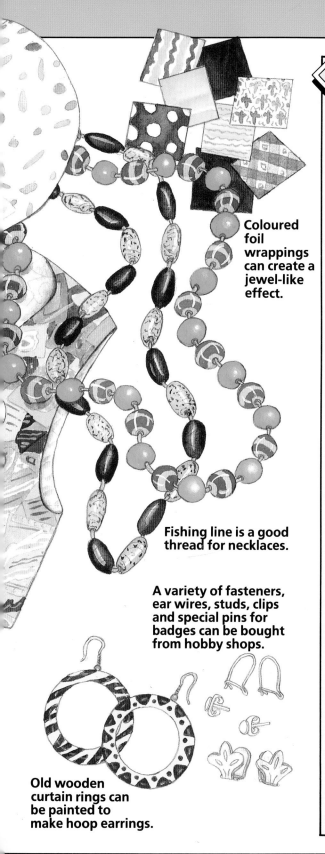

Coloured foil wrappings can create a jewel-like effect.

Fishing line is a good thread for necklaces.

A variety of fasteners, ear wires, studs, clips and special pins for badges can be bought from hobby shops.

Old wooden curtain rings can be painted to make hoop earrings.

MAKE YOUR PAPER BEADS

WHAT YOU NEED

strips of newspaper

fishing line or strong thread

wallpaper paste

needle or toothpick

paint or coloured sweet wrappers

brush

How to make them

1 Cover the newspaper strips in thick paste and mould the beads. Try not to make them too wet.

2 Make a hole through the beads.

3 Decorate them with foil or paint.

4 When they are dry, string the beads onto the fishing line or thread.

Long beads can be made from triangles cut from magazines, covered in glue and rolled up.

1

2

3

4

PLASTIC BOTTLE BANGLES

WHAT YOU NEED:

washing-up liquid bottle

scissors

scraps of fabric old beads and coloured wrappings

strong glue

How to make them

1 Carefully cut rings of plastic from the washing-up liquid bottle.
2 Glue fabric onto the plastic ring, inside and out, and let it dry.
3 Decorate the outer surface with beads, trimmings and coloured wrappings.

MAKE A SCRAP HAT

WHAT YOU NEED:

large sheet of paper

needle and thread

scissors

pins

felt-tip pen

clean frozen vegetable bags

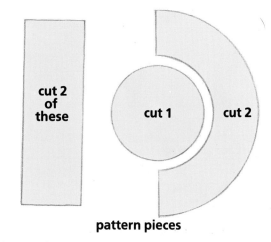

cut 2 of these

cut 1

cut 2

pattern pieces

How to make it

1 Draw the pattern pieces onto the paper, making sure they are large enough to fit around your head, and cut them out.
2 Cut open the plastic bags and lay them flat on a table.
3 Draw around the pattern pieces onto the plastic and cut them out.
4 Pin the pieces of plastic together with the white side facing outwards.
5 Carefully sew the pieces together and turn the hat the right way out. Ask an adult for help with this stage.

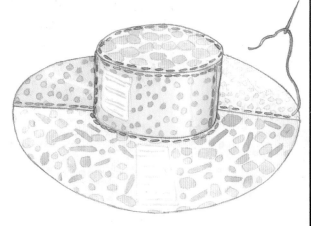

MAKING A "WASTE" COAT

WHAT YOU NEED:

sheets of paper

clean, colourful pieces of litter

felt-tip pen

pins

scissors

clear sticky-back plastic

needle and thread

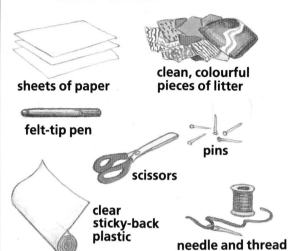

How to make it

1 Draw the pattern pieces onto the paper making sure they are large enough to fit you, and cut them out.
2 Ask an adult for help. Iron the litter under a piece of cloth to prevent it burning.

3 Lay out a piece of sticky-back plastic sticky side up, making sure that it is large enough to cut the pattern from.
4 Press the litter onto the sticky-back plastic and cover with another piece of sticky-back plastic, sticky side down.
5 Cut the pattern pieces from the plastic coated litter, then pin and sew the pieces together.

PAPER EARRINGS AND BADGES

Using the materials and method for making paper beads, create earrings and badges in any shape you choose. Make sure they aren't too heavy! When they are dry, hang the earrings on ear wires or glue them onto studs or clips. Use sticky tape to attach safety pins onto the backs of the badges.

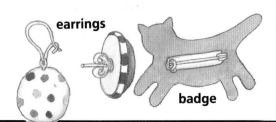

earrings

badge

DUSTBIN FACTS

In Senegal in Africa, flattened out tin cans are used to create colourful briefcases which are lined with old comics and sold at local markets.

The Masai people of Eastern Africa use buttons in their ceremonial jewellery. In Spain, pieces of old tyre tread are used as the soles of shoes.

In Great Britain, people often personalize old clothes and jewellery – this is known as customizing.

THE SOUND OF SCRAP

If you have ever played a comb and paper, or 'twanged' a ruler on a table's edge, you have made scrap music. A musical instrument makes sound waves that travel through the air to our ears. Our brains organize these sound waves into what we recognize and enjoy as music.

People have always made music, but when instruments cannot be bought they can be made from what is to hand.

A SIMPLE SCHEME

Instruments work in four different ways:
Chordophones like guitars or violins have strings which are plucked, strummed or bowed. Some, such as the piano, hit strings with hammers.
Aerophones are hollow tubes that are blown, directly, as is the trumpet, or through a reed, like the clarinet.
Membranophones like the tambourine or drum have stretched skins which are hit to produce the sound.
Idiophones are also struck, but the sound comes from the whole thing. Cymbals and the triangle are examples.
Look at the instruments you can make. How do they fit into this scheme?

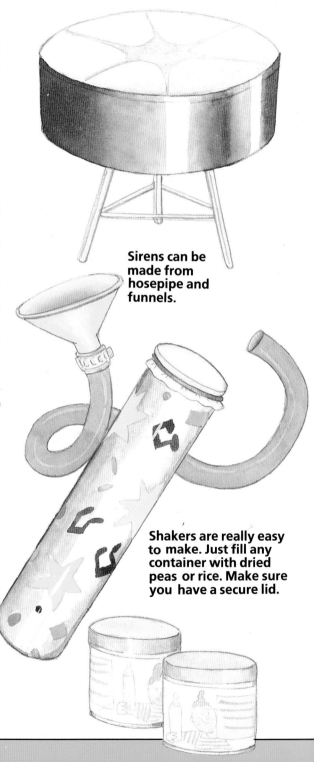

Pan or steel drums are made from old oil drums. They are not easy for you to make, but look out for steel bands in your area.

Sirens can be made from hosepipe and funnels.

Shakers are really easy to make. Just fill any container with dried peas or rice. Make sure you have a secure lid.

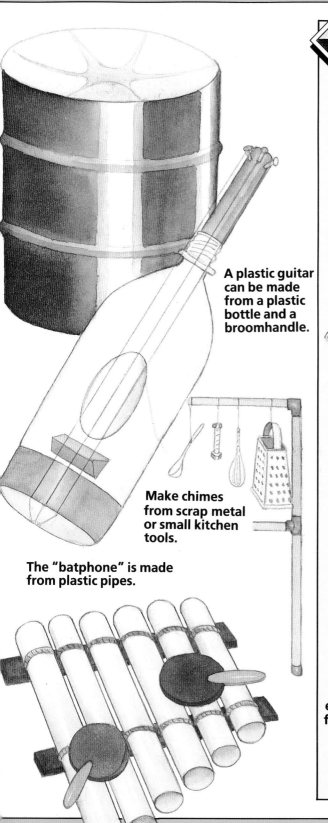

A plastic guitar can be made from a plastic bottle and a broomhandle.

Make chimes from scrap metal or small kitchen tools.

The "batphone" is made from plastic pipes.

A PLASTIC GUITAR

WHAT YOU NEED

plastic drink bottle

stick or broomhandle with 3 nails in one end

cut hole

fishing line or string

triangular piece of wood or empty film can for bridge

glue

How to make it

1 Fix broomhandle into bottle-neck and glue into place.

2 Cut out a hole in the bottle, as shown, and pierce holes at the bottom of the bottle where you can tie the fishing line.

3 Put three nails into the far end of the broomhandle.

4 Run fishing line from the nails to the hole at the bottle base and tie off.

5 Find the best position for the film can before glueing into place.

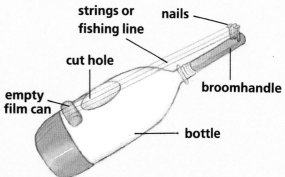

strings or fishing line

nails

cut hole

broomhandle

empty film can

bottle

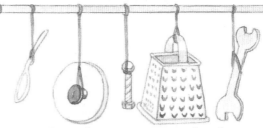

DRUMS AND CHIMES

WHAT YOU NEED

wide cardboard or plastic tubes

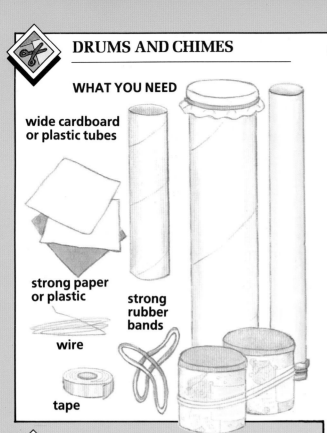

strong paper or plastic

strong rubber bands

wire

tape

To make a drum, cut a circle of plastic big enough to cover the end of a tube plus an extra 5 centimetres. Stretch it over the tube and fasten with elastic bands or sticky tape.

To make a pair of hand drums, use two small tins with plastic lids. You can put water or dried beans inside them. Use chopsticks or pencils as drumsticks.

To make chimes, hang objects like saucepan lids, bolts and spoons from a wooden frame.

A "boomstick" is a sealed plastic or cardboard tube. Bounce the closed end on the ground to produce notes.

THE SIREN

WHAT YOU NEED

plastic funnel

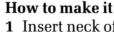

hose clip

length of clean hosepipe

How to make it

1 Insert neck of funnel into one end of the hosepipe and fasten with hose clip.

2 Now, blow into the other end of the hosepipe, making an "O" shape with your mouth. You can try swinging it around as you blow but it is best to go outdoors first, and make sure no-one is close to you.

THE BATPHONE

WHAT YOU NEED

6 plastic pipes (8 or 10cm across) of different lengths

2 lengths of wood

rope

1 or 2 old table tennis bats

1 Arrange tubes in order of size.

2 Ask an adult to drill holes into the wood, so that you can tie the pipes in position as shown. Leave enough space between each tube to allow them to be hit separately.

3 With a bat in each hand, strike the ends of the tubes flat on and make up your own tunes.

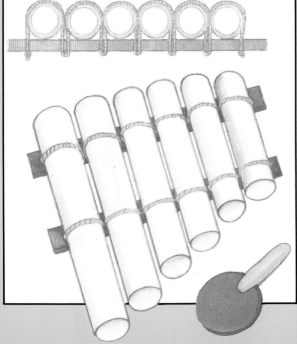

SOME HINTS

By now, you should have enough ideas to start with. If you want more, try libraries or watch out for the many groups that play scrap music. Even better . . . take a good look at what you find and let it inspire you to invent something. Then you can name it and play it!

Strings need to be adjusted. You can make your own tuning pegs with wing nuts, washers and screws. Undo the wing nut which loosens the screw and then you can tighten or loosen the string to get the note you want.

Remember that the note given by a string depends on its length and tautness. Tubes of different lengths also produce different notes. Different widths of pipe can improve the quality of the notes.

DUSTBIN FACTS

In the late 1930s in the West Indies, a man called "Spree" Simon discovered that different musical notes were made by striking the head of a steel drum in different places. This led to the manufacture of steel drums.

"Bamboo-Tamboo" was the name given to making musical rhythms by striking together sticks of bamboo in Trinidad. Can you think of names for your music?

STARTING UP YOUR OWN RECYCLING SCHEME

Every week your rubbish is taken away by dustbin lorries and either buried in an enormous hole in the ground, a landfill site, or burned in a huge oven called an incinerator. Landfill sites can leak. A poisonous liquid called leachate can escape from the rotting rubbish, seep through the soil and pollute nearby rivers. Methane gas is also produced (see page 17). If we incinerate our rubbish we are left only with ash which is much easier to dispose of. But fumes from burning rubbish can be poisonous. So, recycling will reduce pollution, save energy and money and improve our environment.

BEING A WASTEWATCHER

Start up your own scheme at home or school and design a badge to show what you're doing! Before you begin your recycling programme, make sure someone wants the waste you save. Decide what you are going to collect and find somewhere to store your items. Keep your own notebook (see pages 8/9) which will record how much you collect each week.

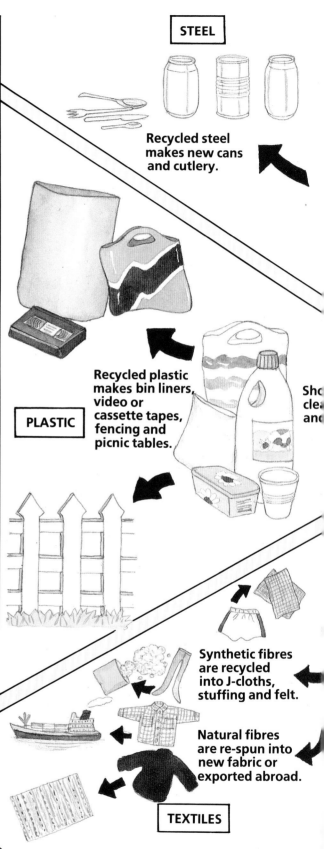

STEEL

Recycled steel makes new cans and cutlery.

PLASTIC

Recycled plastic makes bin liners, video or cassette tapes, fencing and picnic tables.

Sho
clea
and

TEXTILES

Synthetic fibres are recycled into J-cloths, stuffing and felt.

Natural fibres are re-spun into new fabric or exported abroad.

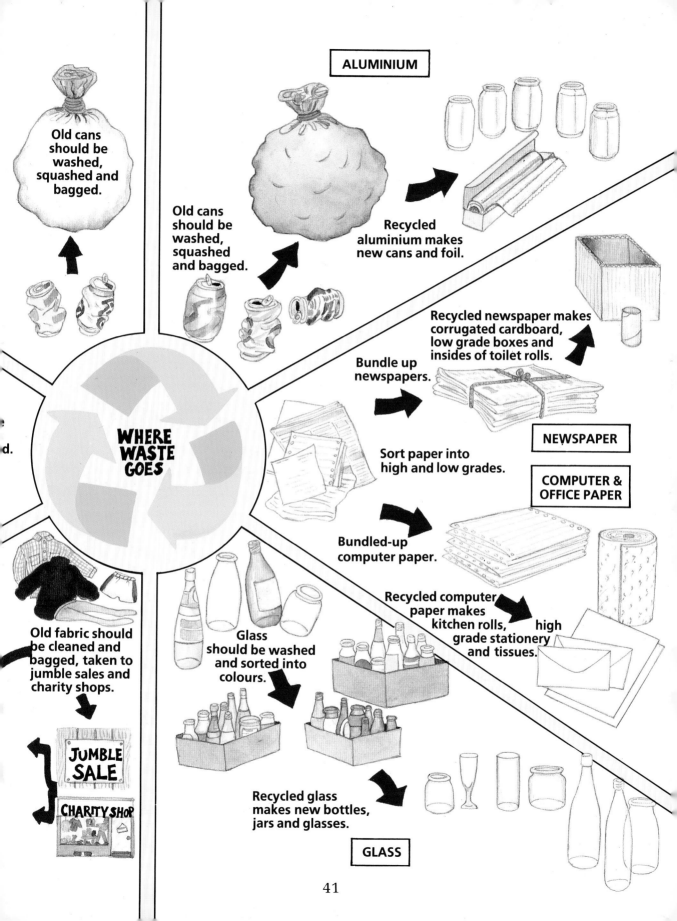

ALUMINIUM

Old cans should be washed, squashed and bagged.

Old cans should be washed, squashed and bagged.

Recycled aluminium makes new cans and foil.

Recycled newspaper makes corrugated cardboard, low grade boxes and insides of toilet rolls.

Bundle up newspapers.

NEWSPAPER

WHERE WASTE GOES

Sort paper into high and low grades.

COMPUTER & OFFICE PAPER

Bundled-up computer paper.

Recycled computer paper makes kitchen rolls, high grade stationery and tissues.

Old fabric should be cleaned and bagged, taken to jumble sales and charity shops.

Glass should be washed and sorted into colours.

JUMBLE SALE

CHARITY SHOP

Recycled glass makes new bottles, jars and glasses.

GLASS

41

USEFUL ADDRESSES AND FURTHER INFORMATION

Recycling organizations

WASTEWATCH
68 Grafton Way, London, W1P 5LS

Wastewatch advises and assists voluntary groups in the setting up of practical recycling projects. It also supplies statistical information and education packs on recycling in the United Kingdom.

PAPER
The Pulp and Paper Information Centre,
Papermakers House, Rivenhall Road, Westlea, Swindon, Wilts SN5 7BE

GLASS
British Glass Manufacturers Confederation,
Northumberland Road, Sheffield S10 2UA

METALS
The Can Makers Information Service
36 Grosvenor Gardens, London SW1W 0ED

TEXTILES
The Reclamation Association
16 High Street, Brampton, Huntingdon, Cambs PE18 8TU

Oxfam wastesaver
Units 4, 5 & 6, Ringway Industrial Centre, Beck Road, Huddersfield

COMPOST
The Henry Doubleday Research Association, Ryton Gardens, Ryton on Dunsmore, Coventry CV8 3LG

Environmental organizations

Friends of the Earth
26–28 Underwood Street, London N1 7JQ

They have a recycling department and can also supply information on other environmental issues.

Tidy Britain Group
The Pier, Wigan, WN3 4EX

Sustainability
The People's Hall, 91–97 Freston Road, London W11 4BD

They can supply information on how to be a Young Green Consumer.

If you are interested in any of these organizations, write enclosing a stamped self-addressed envelope asking for details of membership and any information sheets or packs that they produce.

Further work
The Richmond upon Thames Tidy Group can supply further information on any of the projects in this book.
Richmond upon Thames Tidy Group
Environmental Education, Craneford Way Depot, Craneford Way, Twickenham, Middx. TW2 7SG
Tel: 081 891 6878

Additional information

Fungicide-free wallpaper paste can be safely used by children. Ask if they stock it at your local DIY stores.

Unfortunately the paper in this book is not recycled – due to the problems of supplying recycled paper for the number of copies being printed. However, the paper used is from sustainable forests. By spreading the word on recycling, hopefully it will become more common in this country than it is today.

Most of the projects in this book relate in some way to the National Curriculum. This table gives examples of how activities and text in this book tie in with attainment targets in curriculum areas.

SCIENCE	
Scientific investigations	How strong is cardboard? How long does plastic last?
Life and living processes	Saving energy and trees Decomposition
Materials and their properties	Mining for metals Sorting plastics
Physical processes	A weight balance HMS Recycler

DESIGN AND TECHNOLOGY	
Identifying needs and opportunities	A litter bin Drums and chimes
Generating a design	A litter bin Reusing rags
Planning and making	A litter bin Making a "waste" coat
Evaluating	A litter bin How strong is cardboard?

ENGLISH	
Speaking and listening	Being a wastewatcher Autumn
Reading	Glossary
Writing	Being a wastewatcher A plastic guitar

GEOGRAPHY	
Geographical skills	The trade in textiles
Environmental geography	Why reuse and recycle? Textiles – Raw materials

HISTORY	
Understanding history in its setting	What a load of rubbish How long does plastic last

ART	
Understanding	A papier mâché bowl Finding ideas
Making	A glass lantern Winter

MATHS	
Using and applying	Saving energy and trees Being a wastewatcher
Handling data	Dustbin facts Graphs

GLOSSARY

Aphid a small plant-eating insect.

Bacteria microscopic organisms made of only one cell.

Bauxite the clay-like raw material that contains aluminium.

Biodegradable able to be broken down by micro-organisms into basic elements.

Bridge the part of a musical instrument which holds the strings up from the body.

Cash crops crops that are grown in developing countries to sell abroad for cash, rather than crops which are grown for food, such as maize.

Cullet small pieces of waste glass, used for recycling.

Deciduous sheds its leaves every autumn (opposite to evergreen).

Deckle a wooden frame used in papermaking.

Decompose the breakdown of animals and plants into tiny pieces, with the release of nutrients into the soil.

Developing countries places such as Africa, India and parts of South America, also sometimes called the 'third world', where there is a lot of poverty, and little industry.

Energy activity, or power, to do work.

Environment surroundings, or conditions in which animals and plants live.

Export to send goods, such as cotton, from one country to another.

Fibre a tiny, thread-like part of any animal, vegetable or mineral-based material.

Frame in hand papermaking, the wooden structure with a mesh cover, used to scoop pulp, before it is pressed.

Furnace an enormous, extremely hot oven. The raw materials used to make glass and metal are melted down in a furnace.

Global warming the changing of the Earth's weather patterns, due to the build-up of pollutants in the atmosphere. This will lead to floods in some parts of the world, and droughts in other parts.

Grade quality or standard. There are 11 grades of waste paper, ranging from high-grade computer paper to low-grade newspaper.

Incinerate to burn, and reduce to ashes.

Indestructible something which cannot be destroyed.

Landfill a method of disposing of waste, by burying it in a huge hole in the ground.

Leachate polluted water which leaks from landfill sites.

Limestone the chalk-like raw material used in glass-making.

Litter rubbish in the wrong place.

Loom the equipment used to weave warp and weft threads to make cloth.

Man-made made by humans, not naturally occurring.

Methane an explosive gas made up of carbon and hydrogen.

Micro-organism a tiny organism, usually bacteria.

Mine a place from which minerals, such as metals, are dug out from the ground.

Natural produced from nature, not man-made.

Nutrient the food, or raw materials needed for life. Proteins, carbohydrates, minerals, fats and water are nutrients.

'One-trip' container an item of packaging (eg hamburger carton) which is designed to be used only once.

Ore the clay-like raw material which contains metal.

Pollution something which harmfully affects the environment.

Propeller something which drives a vehicle forward.

Prototype the first model, or pattern, from which others are copied.

Pulp the cellulose raw material for paper-making.

Recycle the process of breaking down a material and rebuilding it.

Renewable to be able to be used again.

Returnable an item which can be reused, without being first broken down (eg a milk bottle).

Reuse to use again.

Rubbish waste materials.

Sculpture a work of art, usually free-standing, that can be made of almost any material.

Soda ash one of the raw materials used to make glass.

Synthetic artificially produced, or man-made.

Vibration movement rapidly and continuously to and fro. It makes waves of sound, among other things.

Virgin paper new paper made from trees, or other plants, not recycled.

Volume the amount, or size of an item.

Warp the lengthways threads that are wound onto a loom to make cloth.

Weft the threads which pass over and under the warp threads, when weaving cloth.

INDEX